MW00639078

To: Michael + Deb
      Wendy + Kim
                  journey friends
                      at Wooden Cross

The Supper of the Lamb

Celebrate Jesus' Special Supper,
   always with joy!

It's The <u>best</u>, and the <u>only meal</u>
that's for EVERYONE,
      with blessings for TODAY,
         promises for TOMORROW!
            Pastor Lou

The Supper of the Lamb

Reflections on the Meaning
of the Lord's Supper

Louis W. Accola

VANTAGE PRESS
New York

Scripture quotations are from the Revised Standard Version of the Bible, copyright 1946, 1952, and 1971 by the Division of Christian Education of the National Council of Churches.

Kathy Corneloup, cover design
Cover Art: Logos Productions, Inc. and Microsoft, Inc.

FIRST EDITION

All rights reserved, including the right of
reproduction in whole or in part in any form.

Copyright © 1997 by Louis W. Accola

Published by Vantage Press, Inc.
516 West 34th Street, New York, New York 10001

Manufactured in the United States of America
ISBN: 0-533-12293-7

Library of Congress Catalog Card No.: 97-90110

0 9 8 7 6 5 4 3 2 1

To my family, who sit with me at the meal table in our homing place, who are so special and loved just for who they are for me—my wife, Kathy, our twins, Katie and Kent, and three young adult sons, Terence, Hans, and Steven, who seasonally join us—in sharing conversation, laughter, joy, and love with one another. From Jesus' Table, the table in our homing place, and at tables with our friends, we are nourished for the day and the journey we share.

I love you all!

For Christ, **our paschal Lamb,** has been sacrificed. Let us, therefore, celebrate the festival, not with the old leaven, the leaven of malice and evil, but with the unleavened bread of sincerity and truth.

—I Corinthians 5:7b–8

For I received from the Lord what I also delivered to you, that the Lord Jesus on the night when he was betrayed took bread, and when he had given thanks, he broke it, and said, "This is my body which is for you. Do this in remembrance of me." In the same way also the cup, after supper, saying, "This cup is the new covenant in my blood. Do this, as often as you drink it, in remembrance of me."

—1 Corinthians 11:23–25

Contents

Preface

This book has been written for guests at the Lord's Supper. The Lord's Supper is God's doing for us! When the Supper is celebrated and shared, the invitation should be to all God's daughters and sons, and participated in for the life of the world. This book is shared as an invitation to go with me on a journey of inspirational reflection on the meaning and purpose of the Lord's Supper for all who gather at the Supper "in Jesus' Name."

This book was first written as a sermon series on "The Supper of the Lamb" and delivered during the 1996 Lenten Season for the parish family I serve, as their Pastor and their Presider at Jesus' weekly Supper. It is my hope that this book will broaden and deepen the reader's understanding, experience, celebration, and sharing of the Supper of the Lamb with all of God's daughters and sons. As we enter the twenty-first century, it is time to let this Supper be shared openly, freely, and joyously for its proper and inclusive use. We need to resolve further, in other arenas than our worship gatherings, our signs and practices of disunity in the one Body of God's new family in Christ Jesus, the Lamb and the Lord.

This special meal, the Supper of the Lamb, is or should be at the center of our community life and fellowship as Christians. To most guests at the Lord's Supper, it is a meal that gives forgiveness today, in the faithful act of eating the bread and drinking from the cup of wine. As a meal celebrated together and shared on behalf of the whole world, and for all people—loved, redeemed, and forgiven through the life and the blood of the paschal Lamb Jesus, it is much more. This little book is about the much more!

A recommended reading list is included at the end of the book for those who want to go through a historical review of the theological issues and practices that have provided the rules for using God's grace meal as a visible means to separate our traditions in the movement of Jesus' followers. As we further implement the new agreements for communion practices amongst Protestants and continue to move toward intercommunion practices between Protestant and Catholic parishes, this book may be a resource for discussion groups. Pastors may want to consider using this book in a sermon series during Lent or during a discussion season on inter-communion.

This central meal in our worship and fellowship life as a community centered in Jesus as Lord is commonly called the Lord's Supper, after Jesus, the Lamb and the Lord of all people. Jesus is the host of this special Supper given to his twelve disciples in an Upper Room in Jerusalem, as they were gathered there for their traditional annual Seder meal. For many Christians, a dominant and prevailing understanding of this meal's meaning and purpose has centered in "forgiveness." The Supper is the visible means through which the faithful receive God's forgiveness.

In Jesus' face of grace, we see our past, our today, and our tomorrow differently. Indeed, we see ourselves as forgiven and as covered by God's eternal yes. Jesus stands in front of us, as well as abiding within us, and says over and over again, even before we hear or ask: "If you have something to take up with this person, tell me about it—she's mine; he belongs to me!" Immersed in grace from Jesus, the paschal Lamb and the Lord, while in a life like ours, from a Cross and through a tomb, our future is shaped by God's doing and God's eternal yes to us. God cares for each one of us as we get to our Easter life in the likeness of the risen Jesus. This meal, with Jesus as the only host, announces, gives, empowers and promises, for all people, what God has done and continues to do for the life of the world through the paschal Lamb Jesus.

It is my conviction that as central as forgiveness is to the meaning and purpose of the Lord's Supper, the meal instituted by Jesus for the Church and for the life of the world is more. The Supper is like a beautiful diamond gem with many facets. It is the facets of the diamond that together give the gem its wholeness in value and beauty. This book seeks to explore nine of these facets of meaning.

This meal shared in the name of the Lamb and the Lord, Jesus the Christ, is a sign of promise how the Lamb upon the Throne of an eternal future will present each daughter and son created in God's image as blameless as we enter that Easter journey and banquet feast-life to come. The Lord's Supper, then, reminds us each time we participate that our lives are shaped by the future God has already prepared for us. That is the deeper mystery for us to ponder as we explore together these facets of the Supper's meaning for us today.

It is my hope that, as you read this book, this multifaceted gem, which we have been given to share openly and freely together in Jesus' Name, will become a more meaningful, joyful, and inclusive celebration meal, at least weekly. Ponder with me in these chapters God's presence, God's grace, God's forgetfulness, God's healing, God's tomorrow.

The Lord's Supper is an ordinary meal with extraordinary meaning for all people, inside and outside the Christian community, on their way to their gifted future with the Creator God through the Lamb Jesus. God, through the life, death, and resurrection of the Lamb, has taken away the sins of the world and given us this meal to share for the life of the world.

Many voices in the world, or from the fragmented Church, or from within ourselves will continue to seek to rob the children of the world of their new birthright in Jesus, the Lamb and the Lord of all. But at no point will Jesus, the Lamb and the Lord, the host of this Supper and our presenter before the Throne of grace, ever say, "I have no place for you at the Table!"

Perhaps Jesus' last prayer for some of us, as we are passed the bread and the cup, simply needs to be: "Father, forgive this one for not seeing, for not catching onto the mystery!"

Enjoy your journey through this book! Participate joyfully in the Supper with others. Remember whose Supper it is, and for whom it was given!

Acknowledgments

I would like to acknowledge and thank those important persons in my life and ministry work who have encouraged me and been the inspiration for this book to take its current form.

To Kent Knutson, who is now at home with the Risen Christ under the Easter promise and who was my professor for the Doctrine of the Church course at Luther Seminary in St. Paul while I was a student there years ago. The eleven Reflections on the Lord's Supper included in the Postscript were gleaned from reading again my class notes from this favorite mentor. Kent nurtured in me my theological foundations and perspectives still basically affirmed in this book. Dr. Kent Knutson later served as President of Wartburg Theological Seminary, Dubuque, Iowa, and as Presiding Bishop of the former The American Lutheran Church (TALC), Minneapolis, Minnesota.

To the many authors of books and articles that I have read on the focus and issues addressed in this book. They have all in some way inspired and nurtured my understanding of the meaning and use of the Lord's Supper. First written as a sermon series, these reflections on my understanding, perspectives, and affirmations are not peppered with names and direct quotes from the many authors that I do not remember by name. I remain grateful to these mentors. I acknowledge their significant enrichment and their broadening of my understanding and pastoral use of the Lord's Supper.

To members of Wooden Cross Lutheran Church, Woodinville, Washington, and members of the Worship Committee who requested and encouraged me to write a sermon series on the Lord's Supper for their 1996 Lenten Journey. This was our way of involving the parish in reflection for our affirmation of the ELCA 1996 Communion Agreements with other Protestant Church Bodies.

To Kathy Corneloup, my Church Secretary, for her encouragement of the vision, her supportive enthusiasm, and her extra work hours to turn this sermon series into a book during our busy Lenten-Easter Season. I am grateful for Kathy's work with me through several drafts and for typing and creating the format of the final manuscript.

The Supper of the Lamb

When Jesus, as the Lamb of God, forgives
Jesus does something virtually no one else can.
Jesus forgets!

1

The Lord's Supper Is . . .
Jesus' Meal of Forgiveness!

And he arose and came to his father. But while he was yet at a distance, his father saw him and had compassion, and ran and embraced him and kissed him. And the son said to him, "Father, I have sinned against heaven and before you; I am no longer worthy to be called your son." But the father said to his servants, "Bring quickly the best robe, and put it on him; and put a ring on his hand, and shoes on his feet; and bring the fatted calf and kill it, and let us eat and make merry; for this my son was dead, and is alive again; he was lost, and is found." And they began to make merry.

—Luke 15:20–24

This book seeks to broaden and deepen our understanding of the various facets of meaning in "The Supper of the Lamb," commonly known to us as the Lord's Supper. We will first consider the Supper as Jesus' meal of forgiveness.

We will begin this exploration by turning our reflections toward one of Jesus' most familiar parables, the parable about a wayward son; a hostile, complaining, envious brother; and a father's forgiving love. This may not be an obvious place to begin a series of chapters on the Lord's Supper. But the parable is, after all, about a banquet. This is a real celebration, with a young fatted calf roasted to perfection as the main course. Today a banquet celebration like

1

that might include polished silver, linen tablecloth, smoked salmon, candlelight, and the best wine.

From the amount and variety of food and drink, Jesus' meal that we are going to focus upon in these chapters hardly qualifies as a banquet. Each time we participate in this meal, we receive only a small piece of flat bread and a swallow or two of lukewarm wine or grape juice.

The parable about the wayward son does not mention explicitly the Lord's Supper. Yet, when we read this parable in the full context of Luke and Jesus' life, we begin to see many connections.

First, biblical scholars today all agree that whenever Luke describes a meal he is bringing to mind the many-faceted understanding of meals in Judaism, in Jesus' own life, and in the families of early Christians.

The Jewish people of Luke's day believed that every meal was a sacred occasion. To invite another person to eat with you was to say, "I accept you!" No wonder Jesus included a meal within this story about a father's forgiving love—a love being always ready, freely given, and lavished in joy without conditions.

This supper vision with the Lord was at the center of the faith and hope of God's people from the days of Isaiah, and before. They believed that on the last day, when God's love would be known from shore to shore, God would put on a great banquet feast, as we read in Isaiah: On this mountain the Lord of hosts will make for all peoples a feast of rich food, a feast of well-aged wines, of rich food filled with marrow, of well-aged wines strained clear . . . and the Lord God will wipe away the tears from all faces, and the reproach of his people he will take away from all the earth (paraphrase, Isaiah 24:6–8). To many early Christians, and down to this very time, the Lord's Supper was and is a preview or appetizer of this great banquet envisioned by Isaiah.

This parable taught by Jesus about prodigals points to the Lord's Supper in a second way. That is in the reference to bread. After the giving of the manna in the wilderness, bread became a symbol of God's constant presence for Jewish people. Whenever they ate bread, they were reminded of the constant presence of God. Luke uses bread as a symbol of this divine presence known to the disciples through the presence of the resurrected Jesus in the Lord's Supper.

Remember here, at the end of the walk with Jesus on the road to Emmaus, how the two disciples became aware of the risen Jesus with them when "Jesus broke bread" with them. The phrase "breaking of bread" is the way Luke speaks repeatedly of the Lord's Supper in the Book of Acts.

Jesus brought in the day when all people were invited to the celebration meal, where the host is also the Lamb, where the host is the meal, the bread and wine of the Supper. The invitation, the blessings, and the promise attached to this meal are for everybody. Yet, we do well to note how the wayward son approached his father in the parable: "Father, I have sinned against heaven and you! I am no longer worthy to be called your son! Treat me like one of your hired hands!" (paraphrase, Luke 15:21).

What about you? Should you have a place at God's banquet table? Do you deserve an invitation to the table of God's food, God's blessings—with the meal coat and guest ring provided by the host?

Have you ever known another person you just cannot stand? Have you ever made a decision—not because it was right or fair—because you hoped it would get you what you wanted? Have you ever been mad at someone and you talked about it with everyone in town except the person with whom you were angry? Have you ever been jealous of the accomplishments of a friend or work associate?

Unless you are an angel in human form, you have done something which, by the Law, should keep you away from God's table—just as the elder brother thought the younger brother's foolishness should have kept him from the Father's celebration table.

In our baptismal announcements, the God we know in Jesus

claims each one of us as his own. God recovers there his "lost" sons and daughters, so to speak. God removes all the barriers that separate the prodigals from him. Likewise, at the Lord's Supper, each person hears the announcement and the blessing that God and his daughters and sons belong together at the Supper—just like the Father wanted everybody, including the elder son, at the party in the prodigal story.

No wonder, then, the Supper of the Lamb, the Eucharist meal, has become the central act of Christian worship. God through his Son Jesus, the Lamb on the Cross of Good Friday, serves as our host at this Supper and declares: *"This is my blood of the covenant, which is poured out for the forgiveness of sins"* (paraphrase, Matthew 26:28).

The Gospel, the good news, is Jesus Christ! The Gospel is Jesus Christ crucified as God's provided Lamb for the world. The Gospel is this Jesus risen from the dead as the sign and source of life anew and salvation for the whole human family. The Gospel is neither a concept nor an idea. It is not an opinion to be argued or a fact to be researched. It is not even an it!

The Gospel is a person. The person is Jesus of Nazareth, God's Lamb in the world. The Gospel is God's way of taking on for each of us the flesh and blood, faith and hope, temptations and failures, abilities and limits of us humans—taking them on in the life lived and lamb sacrificed as Jesus.

Because real sins have real consequences in this life, forgiveness is as necessary to life as air or water. We all have to put up with folks who are hard to get along with, and we all are, at times, hard for others to get along with.

Why is Jesus' kind of forgiveness so necessary? To start with, forgiveness is indispensable because it enables you to live with your yesterdays, your memories. It gags the mouth of your past, which, like some loud-mouthed friend, shows up to tell stories that should have long been forgotten.

More than that! When Jesus, as the Lamb of God forgives, Jesus does something virtually no one else can. Jesus forgets! Jesus forgets so that he can remember the offense no more. Jesus doesn't even seek to identify the offender. That is what the Apostle Paul meant, in his pastoral letter to the Christian community around Rome, when he affirmed: "Now there is no condemnation for those who are in Christ Jesus!"

In Jesus' forgiveness, it is possible to reconcile with a dying parent, to settle up with a son or a daughter who has rejected you, to face a former spouse or a conflicted work associate. If Jesus is willing to forget, it may be possible for you to let go of the resentments, the recriminations, the rehearsals of revenge that haven't yet been released.

At the Supper, when Jesus forgives you, you are free. Free indeed! From Jesus' perspective, you are liberated from your past. There is no memory pointing fingers at you. Present in the Supper, with an unconditional love of acceptance and blessing, Jesus stands in front of each accuser and says: "If you've got something to take up with this person, tell me about it—she's mine, he belongs to me!"

When Jesus forgives, we are granted a different future. It is a future no longer shaped by our past but is now shaped by the Lamb upon the Throne. It is a future under the control of the one responsible for forgiving. Jesus' forgiveness gives each of us a new face through the means of bread and wine. In the Lamb's Supper, Jesus announces a new basis of relationship. Jesus declares that our future no longer comes simply out of our past as consequences or reward. Now our future opens out of Jesus' unfolding hands and gift.

When Jesus forgives, he promises that, as he has taken control of what has happened, he also controls what will happen to us in the future. Jesus will shape each of our futures on the basis of his gracious, free, and unconditional caring for us. When Jesus forgives, we confidently—in peace—go forward toward our future. We anticipate that no matter what our past was and our today brings, Jesus will turn all things to our good in the eternal season of our "bread for tomorrow."

Each time we celebrate the Supper, God repeats his unconditional promise that we are the community of the forgiven. As we see in the parable of the father with two sons, both wayward in their behavior, this is the meal where the God we know in Jesus says to everyone: "Come! Let us eat and make merry!"

2
The Lord's Supper Is . . .
Gospel, Not Law!

> Now as they were eating, Jesus took bread, and blessed and
> broke it, and gave it to the disciples and said, "Take, eat; this
> is my body." And he took a cup, and when he had given thanks
> he gave it to them, saying, "Drink of it, all of you; for this is
> my blood of the new covenant, which is poured out for many
> for the forgiveness of sins."
>
> —Matthew 26:26–28

We continue our reflections on THE SUPPER OF THE LAMB
with our second theme focus: "The Lord's Supper is: Gospel, not
Law!" We are exploring the meaning and the purpose of the Lord's
Supper in the life of us Christians and in the community fellowship
of God's people today.

It is hoped that these chapters will help us to deepen our
awareness today that we are a people living by grace. We are living
anew and daily set free from God's rightful judgment by what God
has done for us and for all people through Jesus, the Lamb and the
Lord. That is the Gospel alone! The Gospel is not our traditional
attempts to understand, to interpret, to debate who this Jesus was
and what this Jesus was able or not able to do for us and for our
salvation.

Jesus commanded his followers under the new covenant to
faithfully receive the Supper of grace so as to strengthen their
oneness with him and with one another as they make real and visible

The Lord's Supper is Gospel because
God is always both the host and the meal
of gracious self-giving through the bread and wine.

this new communion of reconciliation. That is, we—through this gathering at the Supper in every age until Jesus comes again in full glory—are an expression of the community of God's reconciliation in this world.

We are all aware that there are differences of opinion concerning the meaning of the Lord's Supper. These differences of opinion are almost as old as this sacrament itself. Christians who came from a Jewish background stressed certain aspects of the Lord's Supper—such as repentance and the sacrifice of Jesus as the Lamb of God. Those who came from a non-Jewish environment tended to stress the aspects of joy and fellowship.

These differences give us no legitimate basis for using the Supper of the Lamb in our present experiences in any legalistic, separatist, or divisive way. It is the Lord's Supper! God doesn't need us protecting his good news and this grace-meal given to and for the human family.

The Lord's Supper is not just or primarily a Lutheran Holy Communion . . . a Methodist Memorial Feast . . . a Catholic Sacred Mass . . . an Episcopalian Eucharist Meal . . . or a Community Church Friendship Meal. It is, always and only, the Lord's Supper!

We will come to see that all these aspects are involved in the Supper of the Lamb. The various Christian traditions have emphasized one aspect over another—and in some traditions this is done to the total neglect or rejection of some very important, significant aspects of the meaning and the purpose of the Lord's Supper.

What is regrettable here is not that there should be differences of interpretation and emphasis or earnest and spirited conversations about the meaning of the Lord's Supper. What is very regrettable and tragic is that bitterness . . . lovelessness . . . exclusiveness . . . and divisiveness should exist at the place of one of God's given unities, namely at the Lord's Supper. God acts in our baptisms to make us recognized as beloved daughters, beloved sons, the forgiven ones . . . the blessed ones . . . the inheritors. That is the Gospel! That reality and that promise are not based on the Law!

Indeed, it is tragic that in this broken world of ours the Lord's Supper has been turned into a denominational meal, into a brand-name meal—carrying and protecting our brand of understanding and theologies, rather than conveying God's unconditional good news, blessings, and promises.

This Supper of grace was meant to unite all people into the wide embrace of God's good news done for the whole human family. When we participate in this Supper, we are sharing and keeping alive that good news for all people, until that day when our "bread for tomorrow" is the banquet feast of life eternal, when God shall make all things new.

The Gospel-meal for all people should not be manipulated and used by people for the sake of their opinions, either to divide or to exclude. To use the Supper that way is to use it as Law. It is the Law that judges . . . condemns . . . separates . . . and divides.

But, the Gospel acquits . . . accepts . . . forgives . . . and unites. The Supper of the Lamb grants the same benefits and promises to people of varying character, understanding, failures and needs, as seen symbolically in the variety of the disciples around the table with Jesus in the Upper Room as Jesus instituted this grace-meal. As Jesus' action, this meal was provided for and given to all the disciples, including Judas, in spite of! The Lord's Supper is, indeed: Gospel, not Law!

The meaning of the Lord's Supper—whatever its significance for the individual Christian or a particular fellowship of Christians with an ancient or modern brand-name and supposedly with a brand of truth to protect and a brand of grace to give out—must come out of the biblical witness itself. To know what the Lord's Supper should mean for us, we must enter the Upper Room, the scene recorded in Matthew 26. As one enters there, one observes immediately strange language that has little meaning in the world of technology and the Internet: " . . . the first day of Unleavened Bread . . . to eat the Passover meal . . . he who has dipped his hand in the dish with me . . . " What strange phrases for most of us today?

One must recall that the occasion of the Lord's Supper was a sacrificial meal. It was the Passover meal-time for the Jews. And, yes, it was the first day of the Unleavened Bread. It was the time for the Passover sacrifice that re-enacted the deliverance of God's chosen people from Egypt. It was evening, the time of the Passover experience of deliverance from sin in the present time. Therefore, the thoughts of Jesus and the disciples were already moving in a sacrificial context for the forgiveness of sins.

We find in this scene a Jew, Jesus of Nazareth, said to be the Messiah of God, celebrating the Passover meal with his disciples. Yet this Jesus was the One who knew no sin as the perfect Passover Lamb provided by God. It was a time when Jesus sat at table with a betraying Judas . . . a denying Peter . . . a doubting Thomas. They, with their strengths and weaknesses of character, with their understanding and lack of understanding, along with the other disciples, were just plain, ordinary men. They had sinned in the past and would sin again before "breaking the bread" and "drinking of the cup" after Calvary in Jesus' name.

But, these disciples, just as they were, were guests at this Passover Supper that took on a new meaning and purpose. They became guests at Jesus' table of grace as Jesus said: "This is my body . . . this is my blood, given and shed for you and for all, for the forgiveness of sins." I am the Passover lamb about to be sacrificed that God's new covenant with all people might be based on forgiveness—not on fulfilling a legal code!

Now, that is Gospel, not Law! If for no other reasons, we ought to see in this scene that the Lord's Supper is: Gospel, not Law! Why? Because those who sat at the table with Jesus were not excluded for lack of understanding or for lack of worth of character. They were not perfect men who measured up, so to speak, to some standard of the Law. If they did, why then the need of the Gospel? The enfleshment of God in Jesus of Nazareth? The Passover Lamb as Jesus on the Cross?

They were not a group of men at that table, as guests of Jesus,

11

because they had full understanding or because they possessed agreement on all matters of faith and life. They were simply there because of their relationship to the man Jesus. They were Jesus' selected disciples. And, they were there simply because of their need to be forgiven. Through this bread and wine meal, Jesus was telling those disciples that he was about to be their personal sacrifice as the means of that forgiveness they needed.

But the Lord's Supper is Gospel, not Law, for a more important reason. The direction of this Supper is from God to man. The direction under the Law was from man to God. In the Supper of the Lamb, it is not a person offering something to God: his/her worth, his/her perfection, his/her understanding, his/her possessions, his/her praises—not even his/her life. Whatever else is said about this Supper, the direction of the giving is from Jesus to the disciples. That is, from God to man! And, that is Gospel, not Law!

In the first Israel family of God's people, God was in covenant with his people—in relationship with them. That relationship was maintained by the fulfilling of the Law. But, now in the second Israel of God's people, that relationship was established by and is maintained by the presence of a person in the lives of God's people. Namely, by God himself.

This Supper is "the Gospel" because Jesus is personally the Gospel. Jesus is the bread and the wine of the meal. Jesus is the sacrifice in the meal. Or, we might say it this way: when Jesus said, "This is my body . . . this is my blood," Jesus was telling the disciples that God's way of relating to us now is not through the Law.

God's way of saving each person is through the Gospel of forgiveness, through the sacrifice of Jesus' person on the Cross. The Supper of the Lamb is simply an act in which I visibly participate, with the fullness of all my other senses, in God's gracious self-giving and promises to me. An invitation to the Supper and its benefits are not based on something that you or I do to achieve . . . to merit . . . or to be worthy of this new relationship with God. The Supper is not a means for the infusion of "graces" or special powers so that we can be readied or made worthy recipients—like a shot in the arm for protection or cure.

This Supper is rather a visible experience through which we realize God's visitation in the "now-time" of our being and our life to give us a forgiven relationship with him and to give us the mission of being the "bread of life" to others in our world today.

All this is from God, who through Christ reconciled us to himself and gave us the ministry of reconciliation: that is, in Christ God was reconciling the world to himself, not counting their trespasses against them, and entrusting to us the message (the Gospel) of reconciliation. So we are ambassadors for Christ, God making his appeal through us . . . For our sake he made him to be sin who knew no sin, so that in him we might become the righteousness of God (2 Corinthians 5:18–21).

The new life in Christ is established by an act of God. It is experienced with sight and taste and smell through this Supper. It is not established or maintained by the letter of the Law. The Lord's Supper is Gospel because God is always both the host and the meal through the bread and wine.

The Lord's Supper is Gospel, then, not Law, because it is God's gracious self-giving to us. It is an act in which we participate as God imparts grace gifts and promises to us. Its purpose is not to demand perfection on our part in order to be worthy of its reception—for there is always a little bit of betraying Judas . . . denying Peter . . . and doubting Thomas in each one of us. It is rather God's way of graciously giving himself to us to sustain our new life as the forgiven ones in him.

The purpose of the Lord's Supper is not to judge, but to comfort. It is not to divide the people of God in this world into factions, but to give expression to the "given-unity." We are given the gift of our life and the common destiny we already possess as inheritors through the Lamb of God who takes away the sins of the whole human family.

The good news invitation from this Jesus is: "Compel them to come into the Supper!" To compel means to offer the strongest and most persuasive invitation. Sometimes we need a little touch, a little reminder, that we are indeed welcome to the Supper. And that something good and helpful actually happens to us as we participate. It is sort of like those swimming lessons we had—that you may or may not remember, as I do.

The child in us says; "No! I don't want to go into the water! I'll drown . . . and you will be sorry!" Then the child gets into the water and blows bubbles, goes all the way under, and soon learns to glide.

Then the day comes when the four-foot-tall child is to jump for the first time into the five-foot-deep water. The six-foot instructor looks up at her from the water and says: "Remember, I'll be right beside you all the way."

The child jumps in again, only in the deeper water, and begins frantic body movements. Each arm and leg is operating, but not in perfect swimming style. Then, the child's body begins to sink. The instructor puts a hand under the stomach of the child and gives the child a little lift. Suddenly the child is swimming again. And the next morning at 6:00 A.M. the child is jumping up and down on the bed yelling, "Is the pool open yet?"

The Lord's Supper is for those who know that they are often and daily in over their heads in the streams of life. The Lord's Supper is like the purpose of the swimming instructor or lifeguard. It gives the lift, the touch of grace, in the water of living—and sometimes even a major rescue so that we might jump back into the pool of life.

When Jesus said, "This is my body . . . this is my blood for you," Jesus was saying, I am your grace-lift and your rescuer in life. Jesus was saying that this bread and this wine about to be distributed—THEY ARE ME WITH YOU! AND, FOR YOU, AL-

WAYS! When received in faith, they make visibly real my presence with you and for you in your life. Receive me and live under the new covenant!

3
The Lord's Supper Is . . .
A Sign of Remembrance!

For as often as you eat this bread and drink the cup, you
proclaim the Lord's death until he comes!
—1 Corinthians 11:26

The theme for our third reflection on understanding the Lord's
Supper is: A SIGN OF REMEMBRANCE! The context for our
reflections is Jesus being in Jerusalem with his disciples for the
Passover (John 6:47–59).

Many faithful Jews in Jesus' day, from the surrounding cities
. . . villages . . . and countryside, had made the yearly pilgrimage to
Jerusalem at this time. They were there to participate in their most
important festival of the year. Namely, the Passover! They were
there to offer their Passover lambs and to share in a Seder meal.

A young man, Jesus by name, who was on a steady course
toward a special Cross-event on Golgotha, entered the city that day
to change the heart of its people . . . to change the heart of a nation
. . . to change the heart of the world of people. The sons of darkness
could not accept such a figure from God in their midst. Jesus was
removed from their midst by a violent death on the Cross.

We in faith honor that death as God's fullest expression of love
toward us. Here God provides for the world the perfect sacrificial
lamb. As through one person came the fallen condition of the
generations of all people, so now through this Lamb-person comes

16

In this remembrance, we see that God has acted and acts in bread and wine, in flesh and blood, in the person Jesus, to make known and real to us his redeeming love and forgiveness.

the sign and the promise of a life-relationship with God for each person who is without end.

We have a contemporary comparison to this drama. Tragically, but significantly for all people's benefit, another giant of peace and love in our age of violence, Dr. Martin Luther King Jr. entered a city to change the inner-darkness of its people and to change the inner-darkness of a nation. Dr. King was a disciple of Jesus, the Lord and the Lamb. He was walking in the life-way of this Jesus as a prophet to our nation. But the sons of darkness again struck out in violence against God's light for them.

As people of God, we must frequently honor in remembrance—not just one day a year in January—the death of Martin Luther King Jr. That King's death shall be for some lasting good, we must remember it. The remembrance calls us to accept and to act out a way of justice, peace, and unity, with all the phony stereotypes removed. It calls us to express a reconciliation and oneness within our earthly kingdoms as signals of God's coming Kingdom seen in Jesus' teachings and actions.

The Passover was inseparably tied to that all-important event in the nation's life, the EXODUS! Instituted on the eve of Israel's redemption from her Egyptian captivity, it became the standing remembrance of her deliverance and of her creation as God's liberated people. It is quite true that for centuries within the Temple's sacrificial practices the slaying of the Passover lambs, the Seder meals following, and the story explanation of the proceedings composed a powerful remembering. The story and the annual Passover event signified for each person the gift of God's deliverance, in the past, in the present, and in the eternal tomorrow yet to come.

In the twenty-first chapter of Matthew, we read how the crowd along the main road leading into the city turned a festival pilgrimage into a messianic demonstration. They were incited to sing out their HOSANNAS! They were incited perhaps by the disciples of Jesus, or perhaps by their strong living hope that one like King David was on the scene again. They were certainly recalling the great days in Jerusalem under King David during their Passover remembrances. They were hoping for those days to return as they sung their HOSANNAS: "Save us now, Son of David! Save us now!"

Whatever else one might say about the strangeness of the events of that day, especially of a man, riding on a borrowed donkey into a city occupied heavily by Roman troops, being taken as the long-awaited Davidic king who would once again sit on the royal throne in Jerusalem, it was a time of remembrance! Apparently, even Matthew saw in the event a fulfillment of the words spoken by the prophet Zechariah centuries earlier: "Tell the daughter of Zion, Behold, your king is coming to you, humble, and mounted on an ass, and on a colt, the foal of an ass" (Matthew 21:5).

Likewise, in the sounding of the words of institution for the Lord's Supper, we become aware that we are participating in an experience of remembrance. We have heard this reminder many times: "Take, eat! Do this in remembrance of me! Take, drink! Do this in remembrance of me!"

What, then, does this eating in remembrance mean? We get a clue from the meal that the risen Jesus ate with Cleopas and Simon, after their walk from Jerusalem to Emmaus, a journey of a few miles, on that first Easter Sunday evening. When we reflect on the Lord's Supper, we tend to return only to the Upper Room scene on that Thursday evening in the shadows of Jesus' betrayal, arrest, impending trial, and death on the Cross. In the closing chapter of Luke's Gospel, 24:13–35, we have this meal story about the power of memory and remembrance, when Jesus broke bread with two of his followers. Cleopas and Simon—frightened, discouraged, and disillusioned—were talking about the events of the week. They were puzzled over the ending of their Messiah leader's life and the rumors about Jesus' resurrection.

Then the risen Jesus joined them on the road to Emmaus. They did not recognize Jesus during their conversation on the road. And, in keeping with Jewish hospitality toward a stranger at the close of a day, they invited Jesus to rest and to have a meal with them in their house. They assumed that this traveler with them was a stranger in Jerusalem, since he appeared to be unaware of the one topic on the minds and hearts of everybody. Namely the death event of Jesus, the Messiah prophet from Nazareth, and the reports of his resurrection.

All that was left for Cleopas and Simon at this time in their awareness and faith affirmations was "their memories" coupled with the rumor about the empty tomb visited by some women earlier that Sunday morning. This report had disturbed them profoundly, for they had not seen Jesus. Now this stranger invited into their house sat at table with them. He took a piece of bread. He blessed it! He broke it, in a noticeable way! He shared it with them, in a familiar way.

Cleopas' and Simon's eyes of awareness were opened. Their hearts burned with excitement from the memories "this breaking of bread" prompted. Luke reports the account this way: "Their eyes were opened and they recognized him!" This risen Jesus did not stay with Cleopas and Simon. After the meal, Jesus "vanished from their sight." He had done his work through the breaking of the bread with them. Jesus had moved them to faith in his risen presence and promises: "He was known to them in the breaking of bread." So, we, too, can have burning hearts in our remembrances as we experience and know the risen Jesus "in the breaking of the bread" blessed in Jesus' way and name.

The question that needs to be raised again in our day is: What does it mean when it is said that the people of God today celebrate the Lord's Supper "in remembrance" of Jesus? If this were more clearly understood and if the Church—with all her brand names—could dislodge herself from the customary, prejudged conclusions in interpretations, we would have fewer weird interpretations of the remembrance saying in the Supper of the Lamb.

The way must be cleared of the two most popular and extreme of these understandings. First, we must realize anew that what is involved in this experience is not "a sacrifice of sorts." What occurs in the Lord's Supper is not, in any sense, a renewal of Jesus' sacrifice. Nor is it a representing of Jesus to God. Such views or theologies make man a manipulator of God, using the very Lamb provided by God—once, for all people, and for all times! Such views turn the sacrament into a human work to merit God's favor and acceptance that have already been accomplished.

To suppose that "do this" means offer this bread and wine, this person Jesus, to God—whether as the real risen Christ or a renewed sacrifice, as if the Cross-event were not a final and effective sacrifice for all time and for all people—would be nothing short of a grand disregard for God's having the primary role in this whole action, as God has in our salvation. To do this is to put the biblical order of things in reverse. It is to believe that we act in order to experience redemption.

We remember in order to live under the blessing and from the empowerment of the risen Jesus present at the Supper, as in the Upper Room and at the table with Cleopas and Simon. We do so for healing and renewal from the real presence of the One who was once sacrificed for us and for our salvation.

In this remembrance, we see that God has acted and acts in bread and wine, in flesh and blood, in the person Jesus, to make known and real to us his redeeming love and forgiveness. If the Lord's Supper is to be experienced as grace, God's grace, then we must realize that "Do this in remembrance of me!" refers to the reception of the elements and to the reception of God's gifts on our part.

"Do this in remembrance of me!" does not refer to any human work. It does not refer to the re-sacrifice of Jesus, the Lamb, each time the meal is shared. We must never forget, either in the fog of our theologies or in our remembering, that these words of institution stand as a reminder that the primary action in the Lord's Supper is toward us in direction and not toward God.

Secondly, we must also understand anew that what is involved here in our experience at the Lord's Supper is not just "a human calling to mind" of some event that happened centuries ago. The other popular interpretation of the remembrance saying, which must be laid aside, takes this saying to denote merely a human remembering or calling to mind. That is, when I come to the Lord's Supper, I am simply reminded of Christ's death for me and for other people.

In the first view mentioned and set aside, we considered the wrong thing is thought to be happening, namely, our re-sacrificing Jesus, the Lamb. That would be a human work in the sense of the renewal of Jesus' sacrifice or a representing of Jesus to God (to help God remember or to merit God's forgiveness). In the second popular view, almost nothing is thought to be happening. That is, nothing is happening except the operation of one's memory, hopefully resulting in whatever blessings memory might contain for us.

Furthermore, in this misconception, as in the first one mentioned, the sacramental remembrance action is done by us participators—perhaps by you and me, if this is the understanding we bring to the Supper. But, then, the action is not God's toward us! Again, we must remember who the host is at this Supper! We must remember in whose Supper we are participating. It is to the living God, not to us, that this redeeming, this renewing, action primarily belongs—even in our action of remembrance.

So, I ask you this question: Do you suppose that doing this— "this eating, this drinking in remembrance of Jesus"—can be taken to signify for us by participating in the Lord's Supper what also took place in the Upper Room? Namely, the offering freely to all people—even to betrayers, to deniers, to mockers, and to doubters—God's gift of salvation and an inheritance to come, all through Jesus the Lamb who keeps on saying: "Father, forgive them . . . for they know not what they do!"

We must respond, "Yes, indeed!" For, in participating in the Lord's Supper, salvation in Jesus the Lamb is made a present reality for the people of God in their reception of it. Now, I am not trying to overlook or to minimize the truth that, as we take part in the receiving of the Lord's Supper, we do remember, calling to mind the event of our deliverance through the death and resurrection of Jesus—even as those Jews along the road leading into Jerusalem were recalling the great days of King David as they sang their HOSANNAS, and recalled the events of the Exodus during their storytelling at their Passover meal.

However, the understanding that I believe we must capture anew, so that the Lord's Supper will be even more meaningful to all of us, is that, when the people of God celebrate the Lord's Supper, it is and must always be allowed to be "a Supper of grace." It is the Supper through which God's saving, redeeming, and renewing activity continues to take place. The Eucharistic remembrance is not our offering to God, but God's continuing offering to us for "our new life now" and for "our full salvation to come."

Even as Jesus said: "I am the living bread which came down from heaven; if any one eats of this bread, he will live forever; and the bread which I shall give for the life of the world is my flesh . . . whoever eats my flesh and drinks my blood abides in me, and I in him." How can this be? It is because the living God now tents, now makes his dwelling place, in us. God does this in a way now through the Lamb's Supper, with a new blessing and a new promise. We have life made acceptable now and a future to share in the feast life of the "bread for tomorrow" that is for all people.

Indeed, to celebrate the Lord's Supper "in remembrance of Jesus" means emphatically that God here and now ushers into the present the effects of Jesus' past, final, and complete sacrifice for the salvation of the world, and for each of us in its future. This blessing and promise-gift are precisely what was given freely to the disciples in the Upper Room: salvation through Jesus the Lamb!

In the faithful practice of receiving the Lord's Supper, God's people are brought to remembrance. God's actions and gifts through the meal cause the effect of his sacrificial deed in the past to be present and effective here and now, as he makes his abiding presence real with us and for us. We experience and realize, through all of our senses, the visible means of receiving Jesus' presence into our bodies through the bread and the wine.

May we often come to the Table! We need to remember that the living God abides in us daily, even as we receive through the bread and the wine the remembrance gift of the Upper Room, the real presence of the sacrificed Lamb, the risen Jesus.

May something like that happen to us at the Supper. The breaking of bread, the passing of the cup, can open our eyes of memory so that we too can recognize Jesus. Each mealtime can bring to remembrance an earlier time at Table with Jesus, years ago: at one's first Holy Communion . . . at a retreat . . . in a foxhole while on military duty . . . at a hospital bedside . . . at an Easter celebration . . . when a family member's life is closing under the gifts of the Supper and the Easter promise it so freely gives to all.

Indeed, the Lord's Supper is: an act of remembrance! All those meals were times when Jesus became so very real to us, or not so real. But Jesus was the host present anyway to bless us with the gifts of the Cross and the Empty Tomb in our Good Friday kind of world and days.

4
The Lord's Supper Is . . .
An Act of Repentance!

From that time Jesus began to preach, saying, "Repent, for the kingdom of heaven is at hand."

—Matthew 4:17

The Lord's Supper is the meal of the kingdom. It is shared and celebrated as a "foretaste" of the banquet feast to come. We continue our reflections on understanding the purpose and the meanings of our experience at this table of grace.

According to Matthew's arrangement of the story material about Jesus' life and teaching, the first word that Jesus spoke when he began his public ministry was: REPENT! The language of repentance is rather strange to us today, even within the Christian Church family of God's people. It is one of those words that has been dropped in user-friendly congregations, as they have discontinued the use of the Brief Order of Confession and Forgiveness.

The issuance of a call for repentance, whatever we understand the act to involve in our relationship with God, is uncomfortable to some and offensive to others. Still to others, it is ridiculous—especially in public, before or with others.

To many people, repentance refers mainly to that act whereby one consciously attempts to list his or her acts of wrongdoing. Regardless of what the word might mean biblically, in Jesus' usage, by nature we find the word very offending, especially if it means to admit wrong. It is not easy for us to name our wrongs to anybody,

Repentance is the moment of our openness that is responsive to the presence of the Spirit of the Living God in our lives, in our needs and in this Supper.

not least of all to God. As a people, we are not very open or quick to acknowledge responsibility for the situations in which we might find ourselves.

I once heard a story about a little girl who was preparing for a trip to her grandmother's house. Her father was explaining to her why he could not go along. In as kind a way as possible, he said to her: "I'm sorry, Megan, that I cannot go to Grandmother's house with you. I have to stay home to work on my invoices!" When Megan reached her grandmother's house, she explained her daddy's absence in this way, "Daddy could not come, he is having quite a bit of trouble with his conscience."

I imagine some adult made up that story. Whether it is a true incident or fiction, the story describes the central problem for many people in our day as they have rejected this means of release in the Lord's Supper as an act of repentance. Some people stay away from the Lord's Supper because they are having quite a bit of trouble with their consciences (their invoices). They are plagued and defeated by a sense of guilt from their intentional or unintentional wrongdoings.

If repentance is to be understood in moral terms, namely that of keeping account of one's actions, being sure to confess the bad ones, then I imagine that "invoice checking" would and does result in the problem attributed to the little girl Megan's father: "quite a bit of trouble with one's conscience." The experience at the Lord's Supper amounts to this for many, checking one's conscience.

This is the way the Old Testament prophets understood repentance. They commanded the people to repent. That is, to turn from evil or wrongdoing. This implied that one could do this of oneself, if only willing to do so. We read of this understanding, for example, in the first chapter of Isaiah: "Wash yourselves; make yourselves clean; remove the evil of your doings from before me . . . cease to do evil . . . learn to do good . . . seek justice . . . correct oppression."

However, as you read Psalm 51, you become aware of a growth

in understanding of what repentance is. Through some very beautiful words, the Psalmist sings out his new insight. It is God himself who must create the new heart, the new person in each of us. It is God himself who must initiate the whole process of one's repentance. You recall the Psalmist's words: "Create in me a clean heart, O God, and put a new and right spirit within me. Cast me not away from your presence, and take not your holy Spirit from me. Restore to me the joy of your salvation, and uphold me with a willing spirit."

We find this same understanding of repentance in the New Testament. When Jesus began his public ministry, he said; "Repent! The kingdom of heaven is at hand!" Jesus did not mean, "List all of your bad acts, right now!" Jesus did not mean for them to heap up their sacrifices to cover their wrongdoings.

It is rather the kingdom that Jesus proclaims that forms the horizon of his call to repentance. Be open to receive the kingdom! Its presence! Its blessings! Its promises! Its inheritance! That is, repent, for the presence of God is at hand to do and to accomplish something mighty special for you and for all people—as their salvation.

The coming of the kingdom is the coming of God himself, the Word become flesh, full of grace and truth. The One present to do the will and the work of God the Creator for our salvation is the One present in our experience of the Lord's Supper, as we participate in openness to and awareness of the One who says: "Repent! Be open! Turn with a receptive eye and heart. I am here with you and for you. I am your Bread of Life, now and forever!"

Repentance in this New Testament sense is the moment of our openness that is responsive to the presence of the Spirit of the Living God in our lives, in our needs, and in this Supper. This coming is realized, this coming is confessed, this coming is happening in this Supper as a reminder of and an affirmation of God's presence that is always within us for life and for our salvation.

It seems to me that we have seen and understood repentance too much within the horizon of the Law, the Law that judges and

28

condemns. God no longer judges us according to a law, but rather according to a person: "now therefore there is no condemnation for those who have put on Christ Jesus."

Repentance in the New Testament is not that action whereby we acknowledge the condemnation of the Law, but rather our response to the God who comes. We have seen repentance too much as a work of ourselves, if we are willing to practice it. From this perspective and mindset, true repentance is judged to be there when we can demonstrate being grief-stricken and is generally limited to moral failures and lapses.

From this law perspective, true repentance is validated by signs of being sorrowful over not being the kind of people we ought to be as God's people. This act of repentance, then, is done by oneself by pouring out one's guilt through morbid introspection. By so doing, one's participation in the Lord's Supper becomes a means of guilt release for a particular act rather than a confession of our station in life as sinners, yet saved.

What has all this do with our approach to the Lord's table? The Lord's Supper is certainly for the repentant! But this does not mean that it is only or primarily for those who approach with feelings of regret, remorse, or guilt over some recent, new, fresh sin or sorrow. Although this, in fact, may be one's meaningful, valid, and real experience from time to time at the Table of grace.

The repentant then, from this new perspective in Jesus' person and teaching, are all those who believe in a dependence on God's forgiveness along this journey into the gift of an eternal inheritance. It is a repentance through which we acknowledge that while we live in grace as God's kingdom of people already, we also live in sin as human beings. Therefore, we need daily to be forgiven. We need to frequently participate in the meal of the new kingdom. Through the Lord's Supper, the reality of that inclusion within God's kingdom people is announced, celebrated, and experienced.

Although we always go to the Supper of the Lamb as sinners, realizing that we never live full, whole, authentic lives on our own, we must abandon the notion that we must go in remorse or sorrow as our primary or dominant mood, if one of our potential moods at all. In the words of the Psalmist, who gained this insight many years before the Christ-event in Jesus of Nazareth, we need daily—and also frequently—to realize the presence of God in our lives. We need to experience visibly that presence in the Lord's Supper of the God "who creates a clean heart . . . and puts a new and right spirit within us."

The forgiveness in the Lord's Supper is that free-flowing forgiveness of God's under which we live each day, "for while we were yet sinners, God was in Christ Jesus reconciling the world into himself, not counting their trespasses against them." Participation in receiving the sacrament should be a regular part of the Christian's life, as Jesus commanded: "Do this in remembrance of me!" It is not a sacrament to fit only some emotional occasion in which one is seeking release for a new beginning—as much as that is a part of this experience.

We rather come always in faith. We can even come in joy, knowing who we are by the gift of our lives and the promise in Jesus' "bread for tomorrow." We are in the kingdom, and at the Table as: God's beloved sons! God's beloved daughters!

We are people who have missed and who will continue to miss the mark of God's model of the new kingdom people as seen in Jesus, the Christ. Yet, we are a people who are always potentially becoming like Jesus as God works within our lives. As we approach the Lord's Supper with repentance, with openness to the God who comes, it is a matter of knowing or of recalling to which mountain we have come.

We have not come to Mount Sinai with its memories of the Law and its judgments by which we speak about our acts: " . . . for if you mark iniquities, O Lord, who can stand?" As we approach the Lord's Supper, we have come again to Calvary. And to Jesus, who bids us repent! That is, to be open to the coming, to be receptive to the coming of the Kingdom of God. That is, to be responsive to the tenting of God in his people, trusting in the full range of the promise that he brings: "Behold, I make all things new!"

Even now through the breaking of bread and the drinking of wine, Jesus says to us: "Repent! The kingdom of God is at hand! Be receptive! Be open to my coming. For, I am making all things new in you and through you, my forgiven ones!"

5
The Lord's Supper Is . . .
A Sacrament of Renewal!

> If we say we have no sin, we deceive ourselves, and the truth
> is not in us. If we confess our sins, he is faithful and just, and
> will forgive our sins and cleanse us from all unrighteousness.
> —1 John 1:8–9

We are exploring the multiple facets of meaning that the Lord's
Supper can have for us. We shall now consider how the Lord's
Supper is a sacrament of renewal. I hope that as we pass through
the chapters we might all gain a fuller understanding of the meaning
and purpose of the Lord's Supper for the life of us Christians and
the life of the world, the wider community of God's people.

We first emphasized that this sacrament is Gospel, not law. It
is simply an act in which we visibly participate, with the fullness of
all our human senses, along with our strengths and weaknesses, our
understandings and misunderstandings. We simply participate as
who we are in any season of our life, at each meal of the Lord,
because of whose we are again through the life-blood of the Lamb.
We participate in God's gracious self-giving to us, with a blessing
and a promise that is for real in this life and for a place in God's
future as a gift through the blood of the Lamb.

Participation in the Lord's Supper is not based upon something
we do to achieve qualification and presence at the Supper. It is not
based on our merit or consensus of understanding in order to be
worthy of this relationship with God through the Supper. God has

In the Supper of the Lamb, we can hear again and again

"You are absolved! You are forgiven!"

the sounding of the host's words of grace:

acted in Jesus, the Lamb and the Lord, to establish this new relationship with the human family and the whole of creation. We receive to our benefit and peace already in this earthly journey that new relationship of being one of God's loved and forgiven ones as a gift through our "yes" to God in the sounding of our confession: "I believe in Jesus Christ as my Lord and Savior!"

We then moved on to consider the Lord's Supper as a sign of remembrance. Most participants are aware that we are sharing in an experience of remembrance in the Lord's Supper, for in the very sounding of the words of institution we have heard so often: DO THIS IN REMEMBRANCE OF ME! And our thoughts go back to the Upper Room scene, back to the Cross-event, back to the Empty Tomb, back to the scenes of the risen Jesus "breaking bread" again with his disciples.

Our understanding of the Lord's Supper was deepened here by our realizing that to celebrate the Lord's Supper "unto the remembrance of Jesus" does not simply mean a human calling to mind of an event that happened centuries ago. But it rather emphatically means that God here and now ushers into the present experience the effects of Jesus' past, final, and complete sacrifice for the saving of the world of God's people and the creation itself, when all things shall be harmonized and made whole forever.

This is precisely what was given freely to the disciples in the Upper Room: salvation in Jesus, the Christ! This is what we receive today, as the gift and the promise, through the bread and wine of Jesus' Supper. We receive a visible reminder of the grace of our salvation, as well as the actual blessing of that salvation in the midst of our brokenness and need. We receive a visible sign of the salvation gift we live in each day as the risen Jesus abides in us, and we in him.

The question to which we want to address ourselves in this chapter is: What do we mean when we say the Lord's Supper is a sacrament of renewal? It seems to me that this question begs us to reflect upon one of the "lost words" and "lost acts" in most of the

34

Protestant churches today, especially as they seek in every way possible to be "user-friendly." It is also regarded as rather hypocritical by many in the Catholic tradition today. Namely, the word and the act called "confession."

The Lord's Supper is "a sacrament of renewal" because it gives us a visible opportunity to repent. It gives us a personal and community opportunity to turn with openness to receive into our very lives the God who seeks to make all things new. We hear in this meal and receive God's yes upon us. In the Supper of the Lamb, we can hear again and again the sounding of the host's words of grace: "You are absolved! You are forgiven!"

My wonderment has increased over how seriously we take confession today, whether it be a personal expression directly to God, to a pastor, or to a counselor. Or to a trusted friend. Do we have a clear understanding today of what makes up an act of confession? What is the act of confession? Is it the listing of bad thoughts? Cutting words? Irresponsible acts? Desirous glances? On and on the list could go.

Is such a listing of what confession is all about, a matter of arithmetic? Is that the deeper meaning of readiness to participate in the Supper of the Lamb and to eat and drink worthily? If it is a matter of simple addition, what happens if one forgets an act or two, especially unintentionally due to a memory that is failing? Or, perhaps, intentionally—hoping to sneak one act through? Does this dominant, law-centered perspective on confession really reflect the scenes of readiness to receive Jesus' healing words and acts in his ministry or the spirit of readiness to receive Jesus' first Supper by the disciples in the Upper Room?

Of course, there are those people outside and within the Church who believe that they have no need to confess. I suppose I could attempt to prick open their consciences by reminding them of several key passages in the Bible. The first one to come to mind is from the Book of Isaiah: "All we like sheep have gone astray; we

35

have turned every one to his own way; and the Lord has laid on him (Jesus, the Lamb) the iniquity of us all" (Isaiah 53:6).

The second passage would be that of our reflection text for this chapter: "If we say we have no sin, we deceive ourselves, and the truth is not in us. If we confess our sins, he is faithful and just, and will forgive our sins and cleanse us from all unrighteousness" (1 John 1:8–9).

I am not fully convinced that the mere reciting of some familiar Bible passages is going to do the trick, for I believe one must at least go one step further to point out why it is easy for oneself to lapse into this attitude of feeling no need to confess. This frame of mind, this self-image, that sees no need of confession comes out of our comparing ourselves with one another. Such comparisons usually result in our feeling that we are pretty good after all!

It is like that fellow who stood in the Temple and prayed: "I thank God I'm not like that terrible person over there in the corner!" Meanwhile that person, broken in spirit, bowed down, is overheard praying. "God . . . God, forgive me a sinner!" The beggar was totally aware of his condition in life, and of his need for a new beginning, a new direction, a new role in his personal and community relationships.

The essential comparison that moves one to confession is not between one another. It is rather with Jesus, our role model and mentor, the first-born person of God's new community of people in the world. There was a longer period of time, for centuries, when confession always occurred in the light of the laws of God. And renewal was through the sacrifice of a lamb, a goat, or a dove.

Not so today! My confession—and your confession—occurs in the presence of Jesus, the risen Lamb, whose image, whose life-way is both a judgment and a blessing upon us. Jesus stands out in history as God's model of what it is to be an authentic human being. It is my awareness of not measuring up to the model that brings me to confession, that brings me to the Lord's Table of grace, so that his presence in me might be as real as the bread and wine received there. So that his presence might be the source of my renewal. So that I also might hear in the now-time of my life his words: "You are my forgiven one! Depart from this Table with a new beginning!" That is the sacrament moment of renewal! What follows is the way of personal and community life renewed.

There are at least two important points that we must recall in any honest and meaningful act of confession. First, the quality of the confession does not depend on the length of the list. Any more than God being impressed and God's renewal coming more surely and fully because the confession offering was a lamb instead of a dove. That is, in effect, the all-inclusiveness of the list by enumeration.

Such arithmetic only distracts from the gravity of a whole life turned away from divine purpose. Such an arithmetical understanding and approach only distracts from the gravity of a whole world of people bent in on themselves, in need of release, in need of liberation from fear and torment, in need of renewal in self-image and in momentum for living. Even the Psalmist centuries ago expressed this insight into honest confession when he said: "The sacrifice (the means for renewal) acceptable to God is a broken spirit; a broken and contrite heart, O God, thou wilt not despise" (Psalms 51:17).

What is needed in confession is a recognition of one's condition in life. What is needed is not the long list, but the openness of true readiness so that the God who comes, so that the God who is already tenting in us human temples, might bring renewal from within, like deep wells gushing up with fresh life-sustaining water.

The second point that we must recall in any honest and meaningful act of confession is that the need to participate in the meal of forgiveness, or to be open to daily renewal as far as that goes, is not created by our comparing ourselves with one another. It is created rather by our comparison with the pioneer and perfecter of the Way, the Truth, and the Life. It is created by our comparison

37

with that first new person for the ages of time and for God's timeless future to come. Namely, with Jesus, the Lamb and the Lord.

Our guilt is made visible in relation to the image of Jesus, the Christ, with whom we have all been identified in our baptisms. Since we have all become sons and daughters by adoption, it is an absolute must that we avail ourselves of the God-given means to sustain us in that relationship and to bring us "to the measure of the stature of the fullness of Christ."

That which was begun in our baptisms is renewed in the Supper. It is strengthened. It is deepened in the Lord's Supper. God uses special times, places, and ways to heighten what is already real from the gift of our birth and the gift of the relationship announced in our baptismal washing: "My beloved son! My beloved daughter! My pleasure is in who you are to me!"

For our own present good and for our eternal benefit, with our names scrolled into the Lamb's Book of Life by the blood of the Lamb, Jesus gave a new meaning to the breaking of bread and the drinking of the wine together in his Name. Here we have a visible sign of Jesus' forgiving and renewing presence, for our new life now and for the life of the world.

By giving this visible word of forgiveness to his disciples, and for all of God's people, the Church of the new covenant, and on behalf of the life of the world, Jesus was not only saying, "I forgive you!" Jesus was saying, "Let me live in you, that I might make you a new person and your joy be full!" With open minds and receptive wills, with big or little lists of sins, sins known and not known, we participate again and again in this meal to be refreshed, healed, renewed, and transformed until that day we shall feast whole and renewed forever in the banquet feast-life of God's eternity.

Through our confession, "God, we are in need of renewal. Forgive us for not being human," and in the sounding of the absolution, "You are my forgiven ones!," our whole past is approved. The arena of our future is cleared and open. Your participation in the Lord's Supper always marks a new beginning.

6
The Lord's Supper Is . . .
A Celebration of Joy!

So you have sorrow now, but I will see you again and your
hearts will rejoice, and no one will take your joy from you.
—John 16:22

Peace I leave with you; my peace I give to you; not as the world
gives do I give to you.
—John 14:27

In this chapter, we shall now consider how the Supper of the Lamb,
the crucified host, is: "A Celebration of Joy!"

With the look on some people's faces as they approach the
Table of grace, you would think that this was a sacrament meant
only for cloudy days. And, if I dare say so, many walk away from the
Table with as sad and gloomy faces as when they approached.
Perhaps this is because they are worried over whether or not they
really were sorry about their wrongdoings or if God really has
awareness of the one they don't want to admit.

I have often wondered if we have not been misrepresenting
the Lord of the Supper or the early Christian community in our
experiences of Holy Communion. Perhaps it is just that very description of this experience together, Holy Communion, that has
fostered this solemn note about the whole event of "breaking bread
and drinking from the cup" in Jesus' name.

We have clouded the understanding of those words "holy

This is a meal of reconciliation and peace for all people, not a meal for a selected few. Therein is our celebration of joy! We enter into and participate in the joy of the host.

communion." In the biblical sense, we are not talking about a perfect, a whole, a harmonious community of people gathered together. We are acknowledging a communion of people for whose they are—sons and daughters of the host, the Lord and Lamb. The ones gathered for this meal are a unique community. They are a fellowship of forgiven people united together in Jesus for a life and mission together in the world today.

We read a number of times in the Book of Acts of how the early Christian community gathered together frequently in joy and gladness, with thanksgiving, to "break bread" together. Because of their faith in a risen Jesus—the One who was present in the very experience of the Lord's Supper—they were a joyous fellowship. We, too, are to be a joyous fellowship!

Peter, in his proclamation on the day of Pentecost, speaks out clearly on why they were "the people of joy" and on why the Lord's Supper was a joyous experience for them: "The tomb of David, he said, is with us to this day, but the tomb of Christ is empty."

The question that our theme in this reflection raises for us is whether we are "Good Friday Christians" or "Easter Christians" when we come to the Lord's Supper. Certainly, as Christians, we believe that the Good Friday event of the Cross was necessary for our redemption. But, we must learn to live in the joy and in the power of the resurrection, that is, in the presence of the risen Jesus, the Living God, who through love accepts and forgives us. Participation in this Supper with the risen Jesus empowers us to walk joyfully in newness of life, from broken times and acts, while we continue life's journey in this fallen condition.

Peace comes, then, when we realize that we are now judged by our relationship to a person, the Lord and the Lamb, and not by our measuring up to the plumb-line of the Law. This is a meal of reconciliation and peace for all people, not a meal for the selected few. Therein is our celebration of joy! We enter into and participate in the joy of the host. And for the joy before him, the joy in the

41

purpose and the meaning of the Cross and the Supper, Jesus continued on the path to Calvary.

It is a frequent observation to see that we have lost the joyful spirit of celebration at the Lord's Supper. When one enters a church today, during the time of worship—and even more so during the Holy Communion or Eucharist—one is almost certain to find a solemn reverence. Would anyone, happening into our fellowship by chance, sense: Here are people who have made a glorious discovery? Here are people who have discovered in their lives God's eternal eyes upon them in Jesus, the Lord and the Lamb? Would anyone sense that here are people who are joy-possessed?

By the expression on our faces or by the spirit of our lives and fellowship, it might be rather questionable. Furthermore, do we give the impression to anyone—especially to outsiders—that we are sharing here the best meal in town? Have we been, for far too long, misrepresenting the Christ of this Supper? Have we been misrepresenting Jesus' intention for the kind of experience we are to have in this fellowship of his risen presence?

I observe that the most forgotten aspect of the Lord's Supper today is still this note of joy. We must remember that this is a celebration not only of the Cross but also, and even more so, of the resurrection and the promised presence of the Lamb victorious.

Without the resurrection victory, that single Cross-event, among thousands in that day, has little or no importance for us and our life today. Not to mention its significance for our future. It is, however, the faith of God's people that it is the risen Jesus, the Living God, who comes to us in the receiving of the bread and wine. The writer of the Book of Revelation reminds us that our faith-experience, that our encounter, is with the risen Jesus, the Living God, who says: "Behold, I stand at the door and knock; if any one hears my voice and opens the door, I will come in to him and eat with him, and he with me" (Revelation 3:20).

We have been misrepresenting the host of the Supper and his victory by concentrating mainly upon the suffering Savior and the man of sorrows themes. In this broken but reconciled world, we should be celebrating with joy the truth that the battle is over, the victory is won! The benefits of that battle and that victory for us and the world of people is received only through our affirmation of faith, not by our demonstration of sorrow and guilt, be it real, or contrived religiosity in public display.

At this point, many of us are not very evangelical, though we may bear that identity in our particular name as Christians. We are still like the young Martin Luther in his monastery days. In those days, Luther knew only a God whose righteousness was his rightful wrath, his right to judge and to condemn the world of people for their rebellious self-centeredness and their supposed righteousness, believing they had fulfilled the letter of the Law or covered their wrongs by prescribed rituals.

If this were the God we meet in this encounter at the Lord's Supper, then we ought to be solemn. Even fearful! But, as Luther discovered with great joy, the righteousness of God is his right to declare us his forgiven ones in Jesus, the Lord and the Lamb. This is the good news! It is the news rejected as foolish by many people and confused as "cheap grace" by others. Luther had to say, in the joy of a newfound freedom, with the Apostle Paul: "I am not ashamed of the gospel: it is the power of God for salvation to every one who has faith . . . he who through faith is righteous shall live" (paraphrase, Romans 1:16–17).

Even the medium of religious art down through the centuries has not helped in any great way to bring the expression of joy into the fellowship of God's people, for our Lord is most frequently depicted hanging on the Cross—where he was, as physically painful as it was, for only a few hours. By contrast, fewer artists have depicted the greatness of Jesus' Being, that of the risen Victor who even now is present.

It is because we fellowship together today in the faith that the living God is present that we ought to be rejoicing. Again, I emphasize . . . REJOICING! One thing is for sure, and dare not be

43

lost, in the celebration of the Supper. It was from the beginning in the small Christian communities, and must continue to be, a JOYFUL CELEBRATION of the Lord's immediate and real presence.

A rediscovery of this note of joy and the reason for it would do much to awaken God's frozen people, especially in this age of turmoil and increasing violence. It would make again the community of the Supper a dynamic one of joyous fellowship. For all the deep sorrow that possibly must attend the contemplation of one's own situation in life—one's self-centeredness, one's cutting words, one's coldness or aloofness, one's lack of love or feelings for others, one's apathy or prejudices; for all the deep sorrow that must attend the contemplation of the sins of the world, the dominant mood of this fellowship and this Supper is to be the Lord's joy. It is a joy that no other person or circumstance can take away.

For to live in a world where the risen Jesus is our contemporary, in our lives and in this meal, is to live in a world where the Lamb is Lord. It is to live in a world where Jesus Christ is at work, working within us now that which is a foretaste of God's kingdom life to come. That is our joy!

As on the very night that Jesus gave a new meaning to "the breaking of bread and drinking of the cup" in his name—the night of betrayal and desertion . . . the night of denial and alienation, when all the loneliness, anxiety, greed and hatred of people was centered on him, Jesus spoke to his followers about the full joy of living: "As the Father has loved me, he told them, so I also have loved you; abide in my love . . . these things I have spoken to you, that my joy (the joy of pouring out my life for you) may be in you, and that your joy may be full . . . So you have sorrow now, but I will see you again and your hearts will rejoice, and no one will take your joy from you" (paraphrase, John 15:9–11, 16:22).

The Lord's Supper ought to be a celebration of joy because it joins—or should join—all people together under the Lordship of the God who became flesh in Jesus, the Lord and the Lamb. It must be a joyful corporate celebration that breaks down all barriers, as Jesus, "the living water," did at Jacob's well with the Samaritan woman.

Because the host of this meal is the Creator God, who was in Christ Jesus reconciling the whole world unto himself, not counting their trespasses against them, this meal unites in reality, gift, and promise, on behalf of the whole world family, all sorts and conditions of people. To celebrate and to share this meal with any less meaning, benefit, and promise is to make it something less than the Supper of the Upper Room.

To share this Supper with any lesser meaning and benefit is to make it something less than the Table of grace of the Lord, who for the joy before him, the joy of victory for the human family before and after the Cross-event, endured being the Lamb on the Cross. Jesus completed this lamb offering of himself so that the world of people might be reconciled to God and joined together in the oneness of his new humanity.

The Supper of the Lamb is meant to be a joyous happening in which one realizes that the God who is present sees us only one way—as the forgiven ones! In this joyous awareness, we realize that nothing can ever separate us from the love we have known in the Supper offered by Him who shall make all things new and gives us the gift of a new personal life in that future. We are the people of joy! Come joyfully to the Supper of the Lamb!

7
The Lord's Supper Is . . .
Life for the World!

Jesus said: "I am the living bread which came down from heaven . . . and the bread which I shall give for the life of the world is my flesh (my self)."

—John 6:51

A dominant symbol related to Jesus in John's Gospel is bread. Jesus is the living bread, as well as the living water, for the world. This must have been a very helpful illustration in the memories of the early Christians for understanding the meaning of the Lord's Supper. Bread is a central symbol in Jesus' teaching. It was used to illustrate the purpose of his life in a nourishing, life-sustaining role for all people.

In Jesus' saying, "I am the living bread," we have a remembrance:

of Christmas:	"the Living Bread from above become flesh!"
of Good Friday:	"the Living Bread as flesh nailed to the Cross!"
of Easter:	"the Living Bread as resurrected flesh for all!"

In a world that frequently has to deal somewhere with hunger

The Lord's Supper was in that Upper Room, and still is today, a meal that not only benefits those present participating in the meal and receiving its benefits, but it was given and it is still shared on behalf of and for the life of the whole world.

and the shortage of bread on a daily basis, there is something especially important in this symbol. We not only receive the bread, the bread of life as Jesus, in the Lord's Supper; we are to be the Eucharist bread in the needs of the world. The bread that Jesus offers is for all. It is predictable! It is nourishing! It is unconditional!

We are all the guests of God in this world. Since we work many hours, and in most situations for many years, to purchase our food, our daily clothes, our houses, and all that we need from day to day, it is hard for most people to take very seriously that we are only guests of God in this world. We can't create our own eternal future, so we are dependent on the Creator for our "bread for tomorrow," which we acknowledge and for which we pray in one of the translations of the petition in the Lord's Prayer: "give us today, our bread for tomorrow."

We are also the guests of God at the meal of life, the Lord's Supper. Whenever we receive the bread of life as Jesus with us and for us and in us, even through ordinary bread and wine, we remember many things. One thing I remember and confess is my deep dependence on the gifts in God's creation that sustain my daily life and the life of all things.

I also remember our need to be sustained by some gift other than daily bread. We need to be sustained by some special presence and means through this life and beyond this life. We need that special gift no matter how much "daily bread" we can buy, we can bake, or we can receive from our work or from the good graces of others who supply food for the shelves in our neighborhood food banks.

I know that I need often, actually as a daily diet, the bread Jesus speaks of in the scene recorded by John in the sixth chapter of his Gospel. I hope you recognize your frequent need of that "living Bread" as you participate in the Lord's Supper.

When I read this Gospel about "eating this bread" and living under its promise of life eternal, I think about the purpose and meaning of Jesus' meal, the Lord's Supper. This story is Jesus' first reference prior to his death on the Cross to a meal that was to be shared in his Name for the sake of our salvation and the salvation of the world.

A simple meal at table, with earthly elements, became a new meal with eternal meaning. It was a grace-meal. It was shared and given on behalf of all people, while being participated in by only the few disciples. It was even shared with a denier, a doubter, and a betrayer at the table. Denying Peter, doubting Thomas, and betraying Judas!

The disciples were all there as sinners, by acts already done or conceived, or by intentions about to be done, yet they received the special blessings and promise we all need through the cup of wine and the bread shared "in Jesus' Name." The Lord's Supper was, in that Upper Room, and still is today, a meal that not only benefits those present participating in the meal and receiving its benefits, but it was given and it is still shared on behalf of and for the life of the whole world.

A tradition that had started 1,500 years before in the Seder meal was now changed. The Passover meal was now given a new focal event to remember, the Cross-event rather than the Exodus. It was given a new, inclusive meaning and significance for all people, and for the life of the world of Creation, as in the rainbow promise given to Noah.

A tradition of 1,500 years was now melted into a new covenant, there in that little Upper Room where thirteen men had gathered for their Passover Seder meal. As they finished their Passover meal, Jesus took bread, blessed and broke it, and passed it around the table. "Take, eat . . . take, and drink," Jesus said, "This is my body. This is my flesh. This is my whole person given for you!" Jesus said, "Do this in remembrance of me; for this is my blood of the covenant, which is poured out for the forgiveness of sins."

As the candles burned low, and the Cross loomed large, they were the first to eat and drink "the Jesus meal" for the life of the world. They became the first of countless millions to participate through this meal, through the presence of the Living Bread, in a communion with God and with each other that is life-giving today and a foretaste of the life to come in God's eternal future.

The Passover meal the disciples shared with Jesus, the Lord and the Lamb, gave way for Jesus' disciples in the months, years, and centuries to follow to the sacrament of the Lord's Supper. Soon this Supper was shared weekly "in Jesus' Name," as an experience of remembrance. It was a weekly experience of God's gracious love and forgiveness. It was a weekly celebration!

The Lord's Supper early became a proclamation of this gift of living Bread being for "the life of the world." Its blessings and promise went far beyond the immediate participants' benefits each time it was celebrated. It was for the new life of the world. This Supper was shared as a promise sign that the Creation is to be made whole and new forever.

It was difficult for the crowd that day to understand Jesus' saying. Its immediate meaning for them was connected to Jesus, not to this bigger picture of its meaning. An argument started over the question: "How can this man give us his flesh to eat?" This question does beg an answer. Jesus had made a fantastic claim. Jesus does answer the question through the Cross-event and his presence in the Lord's Supper shared.

Even so, this question must have raised additional questions. We still have to ask them, today. Questions such as: How can all of God be present in a single person like Jesus? How can Jesus, as God-in-the-flesh, be present in the bread and wine of Holy Communion? Can such a holy, awesome meal be shared too often? Can such a meal become too commonplace? How can Jesus be present in thousands of other celebrations of this Supper—at the same time, in different places and countries around the globe?

When we ask these questions, and other related questions, we are joining that searching crowd, then and now. We want to know whether there is any such thing as a real God who is really present for the life of the world—especially in these times of escalating civil, religious, and personal violence in our communities and cultural groups around the world.

Recently a professing Christian man told me how he had narrowly escaped a serious automobile accident. He was driving down a busy city street, somewhat unfamiliar to him. He came to a congested intersection. Failing to see the traffic signal at the corner change, he ran the red light. Just as he cleared the intersection, a car whizzed by from the cross street. That car narrowly missed his car. He concluded by saying, "Praise the Lord! God was really with me there! God helped me through my own carelessness."

But was God really present as the rescuer? Is our religion that real, so that we might claim God's presence amid selected dramatic incidences in our lives? What if there had been an accident? Would God then have been absent from that scene or the failure in that incident?

So we, too, ask with the crowd, how can Jesus, as the bread of life, give us his flesh to eat? I suspect that the people in this scene recorded in the sixth chapter of John's Gospel first asked Jesus this question about his flesh being the bread of life because they, in fact, did not want to eat the flesh of God. That is, they did not want an operative God that close, that real in their lives. They were not ready again, like their ancestors in the Exodus wilderness receiving manna daily from the heavens, for a new covenant that affirmed Immanuel's day-by-day presence. That is, God-with-us, as in Jesus, so in each of us. The claims on them would then be too great!

If God were so close, frequently or daily or always, as to be "consumable," to be eaten, then God would be close enough to shape their thinking (and ours), to mold their motives (and ours), and to guide their words and actions (and ours). And, that would be "real religion," like real presence in the bread and wine of the Lord's Supper.

The crowd did not seem ready to give up that much of themselves! They would rather keep waiting for God to come in a Messiah more acceptable to their understanding and expectations.

51

They would rather have God around when they needed him, like the careless driver running a red light. After all, it is quite harmless "to attribute" our narrow escapes in life to a powerful and benevolent Father. That leaves a lot of room and time for a real God not to be around and influential in our values, in our thoughts, in our words and deeds, or in our salvation and the salvation of the world.

"How can this man give us his flesh to eat?" I really do not know how to fully answer that question. I do know Martin Luther's answer. Luther emphasized that in, with, and under the bread and wine, in the action of eating the bread and drinking the wine, we are participating in a witness and proclamation that Jesus is truly and really present in us for the life of the world.

Indeed, in this meal, each time, we do confront the secret of a great mystery: the mystery of Jesus' presence! The Living Bread that came down from heaven! It is a wonderful mystery. It is a true mystery that has hold of us by faith. The presence of God in the bread and wine of the Lord's Supper is affirmed and proclaimed, confessed and celebrated, to be the God-in-us, the God-with-us, and the God-under-us now and forever as our sure salvation.

And, through this meal, all that Jesus accomplished and all that Jesus promised is celebrated and shared anew each time the Supper of the Lamb is offered. It is confessed and celebrated as true: God-in-us! God-with-us! God-under-us! And, as a foretaste of that Eucharist life to come in God's Creation made whole and new with our personal presence in it, we trust the God-ahead of-us! The Living Bread come down from heaven is there, now and forever, as our Life in the world that is and the world that shall be.

As the Apostle Paul affirmed and encourages us:

**Do this! As often as you eat this bread and drink of this cup,
you proclaim the Lord's death until he comes—
for your life and for the life of the world!**

8
The Lord's Supper Is . . .
God's Sign of Peace!

> Peace I leave with you; my peace I give to you; not as the world
> gives do I give to you. Let not your hearts be troubled, neither
> let them be afraid.
>
> —John 14:27

One of my favorite wall-hangings in my collection of artifacts is
made from five three-foot strips of "a nun's habit." Upon the black
strips, a nun had placed a number of different symbols and the word
SHALOM several times on each strip, in cut-out letters of various
sizes and shapes.

Of course, some people do not take notice of it. Or they at
least make no comments about it. Perhaps that is because the word
is unknown or meaningless to them. Others say, "What in the world
is this?" Still others have said, with deep feeling and meaning, as
they gazed at the hanging "Peace! . . . Peace! What a beautiful
reminder of God's peace!"

It is quite important how we read signs. It is important what
signs mean to us, whether it be road-signs to automobile drivers or
faith-signs to believers.

As recorded by Matthew, this is the admonition to us in Jesus'
saying to the skeptical and testing Pharisees and Sadducees concerning signs. "An evil and adulterous generation seeks for a sign,
but no sign shall be given to it except the sign of Jonah" (Matthew
16:4).

Jesus has brought us together into a new kind of community
with all the rich overtones of shalom, of peace.
The Supper celebrates this reality, creates it, and
empowers it to fuller expression.

What is this sign of Jonah? Is it none other than God's sign to us in Jesus. Is it not the sign in the Word-become-flesh? Jesus was God's sign become flesh, lived out among us. That is, Jesus was also God's sign of peace.

This word *shalom*, meaning peace, is one of the key words in the Bible. It has been a key word in the faith-life of God's people throughout history. This one old Hebrew word properly understood, more than any other word, sums up the entire content of what God says to us in Jesus of Nazareth.

In this chapter, then, we shall reflect on God's word to us in Jesus, the Lamb and the Lord, in light of this word "shalom." The word *peace* has always meant different things to different people. Today, "peace" may be to some the experience of being in a space-capsule orbiting the Moon and viewing a place free from daily hassles and the rushing subways or freeways on planet Earth, free from hamburger stands or blaring rap groups, free from crowded, noisy apartment towers. Peace may be a world free from war by forced negotiations where the weaker give in to the stronger, temporarily at least. Peace may be city streets empty of demonstrators or violent gangs, while the causes remain hidden or suppressed by the system. Peace may be the quietness in a home during nap-time or the beauty of sitting near a quiet waterfall, hearing only the sounds of nature.

I suppose, in some way or other, all these situations touch on some aspect of the meaning of that word "peace." Although, here again, we can place a content and a meaning into the biblical word "peace," and Jesus' use of it, that is not intended. This we all must guard against in our faith-life. As we seek a deeper understanding of the word "shalom," we must start by recognizing that it has always been the most common greeting exchanged by the Jewish people, both in the Old Testament community and in the days of Jesus. "Shalom" is still the greeting word for Jews today. "Shalom," that is "Peace be with you!," was the usual greeting spoken between passers-by. It is the common farewell at a casual parting. It is, however, a word that is rich in overtones and in depth of meaning in the Scriptures and to most Jews, to this very day.

To the people of faith in God, "shalom" at least has always meant "May God be with you!" That is the meaning in the Passing of Peace action within our Christian worship services. Like many of the most important words involving corporate relationships, "shalom" has been carelessly flung to one another. It has been filled with little meaning or significance related to a living, present God. This popular usage can mean little other than "Good-bye! Well, I must be going now!"

We are told that mothers separated from their children and sent to Nazi concentration camps for medical experiments whispered as the last word to their little ones, "Shalom! Shalom!" Segments of families reunited in Haifa or Tel-Aviv after the war looked at each other, and then broke the silence with "Shalom!"

Jesus, after he gave to his disciples a meal, a sign, now called the Lord's Supper, by which they were to remember . . . to receive . . . and to participate in the reality of their forgiveness and their reconciliation with God, even as he faced the Cross before him, spoke these words: "Peace (shalom) I leave with you; my peace (shalom) I give to you; not as the world gives do I give to you" (John 14:27).

All this should make us want today, we who call ourselves the people of God, to ask seriously: What is the content of this word in its biblical meaning? If we take Jesus to be the enfleshment of God, as we say we do, then we immediately become aware that "shalom," that this peace, was something only God could provide. This peace is only something that God works out through the actions of his faithful ones. Whatever it is, it is the characteristic of the new era that the Messiah brings. Jesus is that peace-bringer, that Prince of peace (shalom).

To the ancient Hebrew and to Jesus himself, the word "shalom" meant a condition of personal and corporate life broader than the external absence of armed conflict that our word "peace," at most, designates in our world, torn by national narrowness and self-centered religious, ethnic, and cultural racism. Or, the word "peace" may refer to the stillness of a lifeless planet, the quietness of a house during the children's nap-time, or the recent watery soup of the "peace of mind" in the New Age cult in our society. Shalom for Jesus, and the shalom shared, celebrated and experienced in the Supper of the Lamb, is nothing so individualistic, so immaterial, or so shallowly spiritual.

What is this peace, then? We find a description of what the new kingdom of peace was to be in the Book of Isaiah:

> For behold, I create new heavens and a new earth; and the former things shall not be remembered or come to mind. They shall build houses and inhabit them; they shall plant vineyards and eat their fruit. They shall not build and another inhabit; they shall not plant and another eat; for like the days of a tree shall the days of my people be, and my chosen shall long enjoy the work of their hands. They shall not labor in vain, or bear children for calamity; for they shall be the offspring of the blessed of the Lord, and their children with them.
>
> —paraphrase, Isaiah 65:17, 21–23

This is shalom! This is peace! It is not simply the cessation of conflict. It is not simply loneness. It is not being only with someone you like. It is something positive as well. It is a truly reconciled community, building together the fullness of community life in all its richness.

A short-sighted prophet of God, Micah by name, described this peace as every man sitting "under his vine and under his fig tree." But, that is not it at all. The prophet Zechariah, however, properly prepared the world of people to see in Jesus of Nazareth God's sign of peace, to see in Jesus' way of living what was to be a reality in the world of humanity when he described the new kingdom. Jesus stands out as the sign of the first new person in this new kingdom and as a sign of what this new society was to be. Zechariah describes the new kingdom this way: "Peoples shall yet come, even the inhabitants of many cities; the inhabitants of one city shall go to another, saying, 'Let us go at once to entreat the favor of the Lord of hosts; I am going.' . . . 'Let us go with you, for we have heard that God is with you' " (paraphrase, Zechariah 8:20–23).

In this distinction between the words of these two prophets, Micah and Zechariah, is the difference between mere peace as natural man sees it, accepts it, or practices it and God's peace. This distinction is found in our conditional, limited expressions of man-centered peace, whether we refer to individuals, or recognize the reflections of this "false peace" in the community of nations throughout the world or in our neighborhoods and the real shalom, the real peace, as God has intended and has shown to us in Jesus, the Lamb and the Lord.

Jesus is the peace-bringer. And, we, the Church, the people of God, in the world today, are to be a people who live and demonstrate the peace of God as seen in Jesus the Christ. Any sharing of Jesus' Supper in Jesus' Name should not be less than an expression and an experience of this new community of God's shalom in the world today.

In order for us to see, then, what the Church is meant to be for the world, we have to see the depth of meaning in this word as reflected in the person Jesus, who said: "I am the Way, the Truth, and the Life." The first element of peace that must be seen in this expression and experience of community, and the only aspect that we can consider within the focus of this chapter, is reconciliation. We not only hear this message from Jesus. We see this element of peace lived out by Jesus in no selective or exclusive way, which is often so contrary to God's people using and sharing the meal of the Lord's Supper as a contemporary sign of peace.

The Lord's Supper is often used selectively and exclusively as our identity meal, in defense of and defended by our theologies, our prejudices, and our legalisms, any one of which or any combination of which is set over and against one another for determining worthy participants. One can hardly build a case for continuing this misuse of the Lord's Supper into the twenty-first century. Such a practice is contrary to Jesus' action in the Upper Room with the disciples, who certainly were not ready and qualified by either their character or their full and clear understanding, but rather by the relationship the host of the meal decided to see and to affirm with all of the disciples around that table. Herein we see the sign in the Supper as the new peace meal for the life of the world, for all God's people around the table of this globe.

Whatever else the people of God may be in any period of history, and under any circumstances, they must be a present sign of Jesus' whole way of living and Jesus' sharing of this Supper in the midst of people in the broken, denying, and betraying world as it is. For renewal and peace come out of the gifts and the power of the meal shared in Jesus' Name. The Supper must be shared in this way first, with the people in the world as they are, in order that they might become something else. That is what grace is about and the power of the Gospel unto salvation to Jews and Gentiles alike, to the insiders and the outsiders alike, in God's new kingdom and in which this meal is the Kingdom's meal of peace, the meal of reconciliation.

The community of the Supper must be a community that demonstrates and works for reconciliation, or the people within it are like the Pharisees and Sadducees in Jesus' own day. They are still seeking to protect and to defend for God what God does not need defended and protected. They are, then, like the Pharisees and Sadducees who are still seeking for and revealing in themselves and their actions false signs. Such people, leaders, and theologians are revealing false signs of God's presence and activity, false signs of God's blessings and promises, false signs of being God's people, and most certainly false signs of being the new community that God is working to establish through those who have "eyes to see and ears to hear."

59

The apostle Paul sums up this awareness and affirmation so clearly and beautifully in his letter to the Christian community in and around Corinth: "Therefore, if any one is in Christ, he is a new creation; the old has passed away, behold, the new has come. All this is from God, who through Christ reconciled us to himself and gave us the ministry of reconciliation" (2 Corinthians 5:17–18).

If God has loved us in all of our uniqueness and diversity, we ought to love one another. If God has reconciled us to himself through forgiveness and the giving totally of himself for our new life in spite of who we are, then we ought to be reconciled to one another. It is this announcement, this reality, and this action in the Supper that will ever establish anything like "peace on earth, good will amongst all people." It is this expression and this experience of peace that motivates and empowers us toward eucharistic living with and for each other together in this world and on this Earth we share under the one Name we are to bow—Jesus, the Lamb and the Lord, Prince of Peace.

The sign of peace in the world today, like in Jesus' person, is seen when the work of reconciliation throughout the world of people is being carried out in all seriousness, faithfulness, and earnestness. The sign of peace is happening when the experience of the Table of Peace, the Table of Grace, becomes the experience of daily life in community. Or, as stated in a saying attributed to Pierre Teilhard de Chardin, one of God's great contemporary prophets: "The age of Nations is past. The task before us now, if we would not perish, is to build the earth." This is the same message, the same task, that was to be fulfilled by those shepherds crouched around their flickering fire, when they heard from the heavens. "Glory to God in the highest, and on earth peace (shalom) among men with whom he is pleased!" (Luke 2:14).

If we think we still have today in the United States a segregation problem in terms of races or cultures, we should examine the problem as it was in Jonah's day. Yet, the sign of Jonah was a word of reconciliation between God and man, and between one another.

If we think that the chasm between the Chinese and Americans is deep, or between Blacks and Whites, then we should look at the wall between the Jews and the Gentiles in Jesus' day. We must not fail to see how Jesus was God's sign of peace in such gaps of community life, solidarity and well-being. The Lord's Supper must be used to close such gaps. It must not be used, as a symbol meal of God's peace in the world, to justify and to nurture life apart in such gaps of community.

Jesus' life-way and meal are God's only sign of the new community. It is only that those who have been given this continuing ministry of peace, of reconciliation, have not always carried out the task so faithfully, or so well. This is not because they, or we, have not wanted to do so or have not intended to do so, but because our mission has been clouded by false teachings, as well as by organizational and political reasons within the community of believers. We are all products of our culture and faith-systems. We must, therefore, always review and reformulate our community life and practices in Jesus' community in the light of Jesus' way and intentions, including our use and sharing of the Lord's Supper.

Jesus has brought us together into a new kind of community, with all the rich overtones of shalom, of peace. The Supper celebrates this reality, creates it, and empowers it to fuller expression. Our theologies, our prejudices, and our fears can and do, unfortunately and sometimes even tragically for some individuals and families, block and limit this expression and this experience of the Lord's Supper—God's sign of peace!

The new community of Jesus, the Lamb and the Lord, is not just a community in which every person can sit under his or her own fig tree and have life-supporting opportunities for himself or herself alone. The shalom community, the new community of peace, the world community of peace, is the community in which every person invites his or her neighbor to come and sit under his or her fig tree. Symbolically this means to share and to help one another enjoy the fullness of life in mutually supportive ways.

This all leads us to another insight into a deeper understanding of the Lord's Supper. As we fellowship together at this table of God's peace, realizing our reconciliation with God as we experience the Living Lord's presence through the bread and wine of the Supper, may we remember Jesus' admonition that this experience is meaningless and invalidated if we do not, by the power of the Host's presence working through us, seek to be God's sign of peace together in our community life. Affirmed, nourished, and empowered by the Supper of the Lamb, the Prince of Peace, we are to be God's peace-builders and peace-bringers. That is the continuing ministry of reconciliation. That is how we are ambassadors in this world for the Prince of Peace.

The apostle Paul put it this way in the eleventh chapter of his first letter to the Christian community living in Corinth: "For any one who eats and drinks without discerning the body (that is the community of people) eats and drinks judgment upon himself" (1 Corinthians 11:29).

If we accept God's reconciliation for us in Jesus Christ, we must also accept our responsibility for the ministry of reconciliation in the world of our neighbors. God's word to the world, to the human family, to each one of us, in Jesus of Nazareth, is SHALOM! PEACE! RECONCILIATION! The reality is a gift. The reality is God's doing for the life of the world. The reality is an announcement, a blessing, and a promise in the Supper celebrated and shared! Our eucharistic living is to express the meal's reality to the world.

As we make ready to journey into the twenty-first century and share the Supper of the Lamb through the seasons and decades ahead, may we all be so refreshed and strengthened by this meal of peace that in a new and faithful way we become God's sign of peace to one another and to the communities of God's bigger human family. May we be God's sign of reconciliation to one another, for this reality is the only sign that God gives of his presence and his activity amongst us. As in Jesus, the Lamb and the Lord, so in us the bodily community of his presence.

9

The Lord's Supper Is . . .
Life among the Tombstones!

Brethren, I may say to you confidently of the patriarch David that he both died and was buried and his tomb is with us to this day. Being therefore a prophet, and knowing that God had sworn with an oath to him that he would set one of his descendants upon his throne, he foresaw and spoke of the resurrection of Christ, that he was not abandoned to Hades, nor did his flesh see corruption. This Jesus God raised up, and of that we all are witnesses. Being therefore exalted at the right hand of God, and having received from the Father the promise of the Holy Spirit, he has poured out this which you see and hear.

—Peter's Word: Acts 2:29–33

In the Supper of the Lamb, all creation has already been transformed through the servant-love and life-giving of Jesus. Through this Supper we join Jesus in his journey from birth . . . through life's ways and needs . . . to an Upper Room Seder meal for the Passover . . . out into the places of our struggles and our choices symbolized in the Garden of Gethsemane . . . to his tombstone place . . . unto life risen new and whole forever.

The eating and drinking of this meal, with a new focal person and event, is again holy. Its object is no longer the food, but the presence of the Living Lamb, the God of Creation. In this meal of servant-love, where the host is both the Lamb and the Victor, our

The promise in the Lamb's Supper takes us through a tomb, Jesus' tomb, that is empty. This meal is always an Easter meal, an Easter happening.

faith becomes concrete. It becomes carnal. In this eating and drinking, we participate in the passion story of Jesus, lived for all people, with its focus on the death and the resurrection of the first-born of God's new Creation, Jesus the Christ.

There is a tradition that tells us that long ago it was the fervent desire of the faithful to be buried near the graves of the martyrs. When people of means died, they provided for large amounts of food to be placed on their graves. It was expected that the poor and hungry would visit the graves and eat and drink in the presence of the departed. It was expected that they would offer prayers to the God of Creation on behalf of the departed. And in eating and drinking and praying in the midst of the tombstones, life would go on—on this side of eternity and on the other side.

When Jesus shared the first Supper of the Lamb, Jesus assured his disciples that he would not stay in the tomb. On the third day, he would rise. And, then, he would be their eternal host, amidst the tombstones in this life and in the Easter life to come for all who have journeyed along Earth's way.

What Jesus wanted his disciples to know in that Upper Room, Jesus acted out in the washing of the disciples' feet. The servant host of Creation and the host of the Supper of the Lamb are one and the same, the God of unconditional and limitless love. At the beginning and in the end of time as we mark it, at the altar, in the places of tombstones, until the final banquet, all of life is Eucharist, is life from God.

Every time we eat this bread and drink of this cup in Jesus' Name, we are doing so for "the life of the world." We do not participate just for ourselves or because we recognize our personal brokenness and wrongdoings. The cup and the bread were served to all of the disciples around the table, whether they fully under-stood or not, in spite of their actions of doubt, denial, and betrayal.

We see along Jesus' way with the disciples and in the Upper Room that there are many tomb experiences or realities in life—even among the living, for a tomb symbol can signify more than a burying place for the dead. Along his servant life for others, Jesus was the Life, the Light, the Living Bread amidst their tombs of self-righteousness, greed, and racism; amidst their doubts, denials, and betrayals.

We can choose to live life daily in captivating tombs, to go to tombs, or be inside of tombs. We can affirm the illusion of being a self-made savior. Or we can respond to the story of Jesus' tomb visit by three women and proclaim: Jesus is risen! Jesus is alive to make all things new! We can choose a different point of view . . . a different perspective . . . a different reality and hope with which to live.

The promise in the Lamb's Supper takes us through a tomb, Jesus' tomb, which is empty. This meal is always an Easter meal, an Easter happening. My dying and my rising with Jesus not only comfort and refresh me, so that I, along with Jesus, can face and encounter life's Cross necessities and happenings without a mumbling word, they empower me to live day by day with strength and joy as a death-transcending, a tomb-transcending, person—for "those clothed in the garment gift of Jesus' righteousness and living presence have already become new."

As we have journeyed through these reflections, we have been proclaiming that Jesus as the Lamb is a "testament of God's love for us." That testament of love has been proclaimed to us through the words from Peter and Paul. Love is the number one characteristic of the Supper of the Lamb and of the Christian faith. God is love! And those who abide in love, abide in God, and God abides clearly in them!

For this particular Passover, Jesus rode into Jerusalem on a donkey, a sign of servant-love. No king rides on a donkey. But Jesus did as the Lamb to be sacrificed on the Cross for the human family. As you know, the crowds put palm branches on the road and waved them, shouting: "Hosanna! Blessed is he who comes in the name of the Lord!" But as the week moved on, Jesus drew closer to the

Holy City and wept, and said, "Would that even today you knew the things that make for peace!"

Then Jesus moved to the Upper Room, the Upper Room of sacrament and servant-love. In his Supper with his disciples, Jesus said to them: "I give you a new commandment, that you love one another, even as I have loved you."

Jesus had to face the fear of utter rejection, and death itself, just days after the shouting of the hosannas. Out of the wrestling struggle in Gethsemane, Jesus went forth again to affirm the way for which he was born into this world, the way of servant-love, even unto the Cross and through the Tomb.

It is told that Mother Teresa once said, "Our vocation is to belong to Jesus with the conviction that nothing and nobody can separate us from the love of Christ. . . . God loves the world through us. Just as God sent Jesus to be his love, his presence in the world, so today God is sending us to love. Really God is very much in love with us, and that is why Jesus continually says, 'Love as I have loved you.' " Indeed, we have been put personally into Jesus' passion story of servant-love by the splashing of water, and kept there through a cup of wine and bread shared in the risen Jesus' Name—with a Cross and an empty tomb in the center of it all!

Just as a flower seed must die to rise in beauty once again, Jesus died and rose in glory as servant-love, bringing us the sign and the promise of Easter-life each time we break the bread and share the cup in the Supper of the Lamb. Come to the Supper! Jesus is alive for you! We are alive together in Jesus, forever! Blessed by the Lamb, our servant host, we are called to the way of servant-love in our eucharistic living with and for one another.

10
Postscript:
Eleven Reflections on the Lord's Supper

> . . .the Lord Jesus on the night when he was betrayed took
> bread, and when he had given thanks, he broke it, and said,
> "This is my body which is for you. DO THIS IN REMEM-
> BRANCE OF ME." In the same way also the cup, after supper,
> saying, "This cup is the new covenant in my blood. DO THIS,
> AS OFTEN AS YOU DRINK IT, IN REMEMBRANCE OF
> ME." For as often as you eat this bread and drink the cup, you
> proclaim the Lord's death until he comes.
> —1 Corinthians 11:23–26

1. The Lord's Supper is **GOSPEL,** not law. It is God's gracious
   gift of forgiveness to us. Its purpose is not to demand perfection on our part to be worthy of its reception, but rather God's
   way of graciously giving Himself to us to sustain our new life
   as the forgiven ones in Him. The purpose of the Lord's Supper
   is not to judge, but to comfort; not to divide the people of
   God in the human family, but to unite; not to fill our hearts
   with terror, but with joy.

2. The Lord's Supper is **A SIGN.** It is a visible sign of God's
   gracious will toward all people—to forgive them. It is a visible
   sign to the person of faith that God is personally present. It
   is a sign of remembrance: of the blood of the Cross shed for
   us . . . of Jesus as the true bread of life given for us . . . of the

suffering on the Cross for us . . . and of the banquet feast yet to come.

3. The Lord's Supper is **A SACRAMENT OF RENEWAL.** It is termed a sacrament of renewal of our life in God, while baptism was the sacrament by which we were initiated into this new life in God. That which was begun in our baptisms is strengthened, deepened, and renewed in the Lord's Supper.

4. The Lord's Supper is **PARTICIPATION** in the community of Jesus' followers. It involves not only communion with the personal presence of Jesus, our Lord and Savior, but also a witness of the fellowship that should exist among the individuals who are followers of the Lord of life.

5. The Lord's Supper is **A MEMORIAL FEAST.** The same person who lived, died, and arose for our new life now and for our eternal life is the one who comes to us through the bread and wine. The Lord's Supper identifies the community of Christ in the world today, a community of faith in Him as Lord and Savior that arose out of the event of the Cross and the resurrection. As we participate in this supper, we identify ourselves with all of Christ's own people who have gathered in the fellowship of this sacrament down through the centuries.

6. The Lord's Supper is **AN ACT OF CONFESSION.** Knowing ourselves and our need of renewal through forgiveness, we go to meet Him through this visible and more dramatic way, as we also meet Him in His Word and in our lives and the lives of others each day. It is still His action . . . His Supper, but we go in boldness to the table of grace. The initiative is now ours as much as His. We do something here, too: "WE MUST GO." Why? Because He invites and He waits for our coming. And, in so going, we witness to His life, death, and resurrection for us. This act of our going is not a meritorious work, but we must decide. We must go as a response to the invitation.

7. The Lord's Supper is **A SACRAMENT OF REPEN-TANCE.** It is for the penitent, but the sacrament does not have a psychological demand of some fresh sin to confess before one needs to come. It is a repentance that we acknow-ledge that, while we live in grace, we also live in sin. The penitent are all who believe in a dependence on God's forgiveness in life. We must not go in remorse to the Lord's Supper, though we always do as sinners. We should rather always go as sinners who are already justified as the forgiven ones in Jesus Christ and who trust joyfully in what one receives in the sacrament. The Lord's Supper is not a sacra-ment to fit only emotional needs once in awhile; it should be a regular part of the Christian life. DO THIS IN REMEM-BRANCE OF ME!

8. The Lord's Supper is **A SACRAMENT OF JOY.** We so often forget this aspect—the celebration of joy. This is a celebration not only of the Cross but also of the resurrection. It is the Risen Christ, the living God, who comes to us in the receiving of bread and wine.

9. The Lord's Supper is **A SACRAMENT OF THE CON-TINUED CHRISTIAN LIFE.** God is always present in this church, that is, in His people, and not only in the sacrament. The effects of the sacrament are not confined to the moment but go on into the future. Thus, we do not believe that we must have the sacrament every day to live in God's grace. On the other hand, we ought to frequently accept Jesus' invita-tion: DO THIS, AS OFTEN AS YOU DO IT, IN REMEM-BRANCE OF ME!

10. The Lord's Supper is **THE MODE OF HIS BODY AND BLOOD.** There is a point of mystery here of grace and faith. The personal presence of Jesus in the experience of the sacrament must be accepted in the simplicity of faith. It is an act of confessing His presence for the forgiveness of sin. It is not an act on our part that should demand a scientific

explanation of "the how?". We come in faith with the expectation of meeting Him and knowing that we are the forgiven ones.

11. The Lord's Supper is **A SACRAMENT OF HOPE.** As we come we remember the past events of His life, death, and resurrection for us in the present experience of the sacrament. And we look forward in hope to that which is promised to come. That which is not yet completed in God's New Creation is celebrated now, enjoyed now, and experienced now, as a foretaste of the fellowship and communion with God and one another that will continue in the resurrection.

Recommended Reading

Abbott, Walter M., S. J., general editor. *The Document of Vatican II.* (With Notes and Comments by Catholic, Protestant, and Orthodox Authorities.) New York: Guild Press, 1966.

Anderson, J. George, T. Austin Murphy, and Joseph A. Burgess, editors. *Justification by Faith, Lutherans and Catholics in Dialogue VII.* Minneapolis: Augsburg Publishing House, 1985.

Balasuriya, Tissa. *The Eucharist and Human Liberation.* New York: Orbis Books, 1979.

Cullman, Oscar and Leenhardt, F. J., *Essays on the Lord's Supper. Ecumenical Studies on Worship* no. 1. Translated by J. G. Davies. Richmond, Virginia: John Knox Press, 1963.

Hellwig, Monika K. *The Eucharist and the Hunger of the World.* New York: Paulist Press/Dens Books, 1976.

Lazareth, William H. *Growing Together in Baptism, Eucharist and Ministry: A Study Guide.* (For Faith and Order Paper no. III, *Baptism, Eucharist and Ministry,* Geneva; World Council of Churches, 1982). Faith and Order Paper no. 114. Geneva: World Council of Churches, 1982.

Lehmann, H. T., editor. *Meaning and Practice of the Lord's Supper.* Philadelphia: Muhlenberg Press, 1961.

Marty, Martin. *The Lord's Supper.* Philadelphia: Fortress Press, 1962.

McCormich, Scott, Jr. *The Lord's Supper: A Biblical Interpretation.* Philadelphia: Westminster Press, 1966.

Nicholas, Marie-Joseph, O.P. *A New Look at the Eucharist. (What Is the Eucharist?)* Translated from the French by Reninald F. Trevett. Glen Rock, New Jersey: Paulist Press/Dens Books, 1964.

Schillebeeckx, E., O. P. *The Eucharist.* Translated by N. D. Smith. New York: Sheed and Ward, 1968.

Stewart, E. M., translator. *The Eucharist in the New Testament.* (A symposium.) Baltimore: Helicon Press, 1965.

Tappert, Theodore G. *The Lord's Supper (Past and Present Practices).* Philadelphia: Muhlenberg Press, 1961.

Lutheran and Catholics in Dialogue IV: Eucharist and Ministry. New York: Representatives of the U.S.A. National Committee of the Lutheran World Federation and the Bishops' Committee for Ecumenical and Interreligious Affairs, 1970.